THE INFLUENTIAL DOCTOR

THE INFLUENTIAL DOCTOR

HOW TO ATTRACT & RETAIN YOUR PREFERRED PATIENTS AND BUILD A PROFITABLE PRACTICE THAT MATTERS

JR BURGESS
CEO HealthOvators

Niche Pressworks

Indianapolis

THE INFLUENTIAL DOCTOR

For more information, visit HealthOvators; **HealthOvators.com**

Published by Niche Pressworks; **NichePressworks.com**

CONTENTS

INTRODUCTION

WE'VE GOT TO CHANGE HEALTHCARE

The healthcare system in our country is convoluted and broken.

I'm sure that's no surprise to you.

What may be a surprise to you is just how achievable it is to break free and have an independent, profitable business that allows you to practice integrated and regenerative health care unrestricted by hospital boards, insurance companies, and pharmaceuticals.

Freedom from an obsolete model that rewards managing symptoms instead of eliminating them; covering up problems instead of resolving root causes; and all too often, causing more harm than good.

The good news is, there is another model. A model that allows you to spend more meaningful time with your patients and develop an effective protocol that you can feel good about prescribing.

A model that lets you see half the patients while earning more income, all without dealing with insurance, bureaucracy, or red tape.

A business that empowers you to practice life-changing medicine for cash-paying patients who are happy to pull out their wallets in exchange for real solutions.

But first, let me tell you how I discovered this model.

A CHANCE ENCOUNTER

I met Dr. Baumgartner the last day our community's clinic was in business. The decision-makers were shutting down the local center and centralizing operations in a bigger city. Dr. Baumgartner made the courageous decision to keep his family where they were and open his own independent practice instead.

I was a trainer at Gold's Gym, and he stopped in that day to observe me training one of his patients. His patient, Geoff, had a torn rotator cuff. We chatted about my chronic pain issues and how Dr. Baumgartner had fixed Geoff's shoulder without surgery.

I was turning thirty years old and already had five knee surgeries. My weekend passion was playing rugby, even though I had a constant, painful limp. I needed to give up the sport, but the aggressive and competitive aspect of rugby was my greatest relief and outlet for handling my emotions.

Dr. Baumgartner offered me a unique solution if I would come see him at his new office.

I was willing to try anything to keep playing the game I loved and obliged. After two treatments, my leg pain was completely gone.

To say I was shocked and deeply grateful would be an understatement. He transformed my life when every other doctor I visited only treated the symptoms.

Dr. Baumgartner's approach was different. He was passionate about providing safe, minimally invasive procedures that are effective at eliminating (or drastically reducing) pain and injuries without drugs or surgery as the first-line treatment.

Because I was a trainer who ate healthily and exercised, he showed me why I experienced faster results than a typical patient. My lifestyle habits were a key factor in my success, and that benefited us both.

The next offer out of his mouth surprised me even more. "I need someone in my business who can help me add a concierge lifestyle and preventative medicine component. Would you be willing to join us and transform even more lives?"

Back then, I was watching a lot of 'The Biggest Loser,' imagining it as my dream job. I thought, *'If only I could lock people in a cabin for a month, I could help them overcome their unhealthy lifestyles and change their new behaviors until it became habitual.'*

Dr. Baumgartner was willing to take any measures possible to make it happen, but he needed help completing his model. He also envisioned someone helping him change the world of healthcare for doctors and patients everywhere. I was all in!

Neither of us knew much about marketing and attracting clients at the time, but we knew we needed clients fast. Dr. Baumgartner sent me to every marketing and sales event, class, and course I could possibly attend.

I studied and applied marketing ideas from the best experts in the business.

What I learned helped us grow rapidly. It also kept us from failing five years later when we built a brand-new 28,000 square foot integrated health center and unexpectedly lost all our insurance contracts. Insurers refused to cover us because we would not give up functional medicine, stem cells, and platelet-rich plasma injections (PRP).

Contrary to popular belief, we discovered we could survive and thrive as a business without insurance companies paying the bills.

Our marketing and sales process were key.

We used marketing to attract professional athletes, celebrities, and influencers who were willing to pay for results. We leveraged the results we got from these well-known people and asked them to share their success stories.

Their influence lead to a significant increase in everyday patients who were excited that there was hope for their loved ones or themselves.

Dr. Baumgartner and I became recognized and sought after in the medical and fitness world, and our Rejuv Medical Center was a proving ground for a new type of healthcare model.

The more we grew, the more excited we got about helping other practices do the same thing. We started speaking on national stages and hosting workshops and seminars to teach other doctors what we were doing.

Then their success rates increased. As we learned and taught, we fine-tuned and enhanced the model to best serve our doctor clients and developed a system that could bring them consistent and predictable results.

Eventually, we'd honed it down to what we call our "5 Pillars of Practice Success Program".

After ten years of steady growth, Dr. Baumgartner and I were established enough to go our own ways. I let go of my role as CEO of Rejuv to focus solely on helping medical professionals restore and regenerate health.

That is where HealthOvators began. Now I travel the world doing what I do best: speaking, coaching, and creating next-level healthcare models that will change the world.

My goal is to show you the marketing and sales techniques that work for us and the doctors we've helped.

These ideas have been proven successful in all types of communities—from big cities where competing alternatives are literally next door to one another, to rural communities with populations so low their profits defy expectations.

We built one of the top regenerative medicine clinics in the world in Waite Park, Minnesota, where the median household income is $45,000 per year.

If we did that there, you can do this wherever you are.

START WHERE YOU ARE

This book is for physicians, practice owners, and wellness professionals who want to help patients restore and regenerate health without drugs and surgery as the first-line treatment. Doctors who offer cash-pay services such as regenerative medicine, functional medicine, weight loss, and lifestyle medicine.

If you want to build a proven model of healthcare that is outcome-driven, affordable, sustainable, and profitable, I want to help you do that.

At HealthOvators, we are on a mission to redefine healthcare through medical practices, wellness centers, fitness facilities, and/or online health programs focused on delivering remarkable outcomes.

We have all the systems, processes, and protocols you need to build a successful business no matter where you are right now.

In this short book, we're going to focus on marketing and sales because when you know how to create a steady stream of incoming and recurring revenue...anything and everything is possible.

The independence, influence, impact, and income you want are achievable.

We've done it. Let me show you how to become the influential doctor people will pay any price to see.

I have one prerequisite:

You don't have my permission to use these secrets if you don't get great outcomes for your patients.

It's okay if you're just now discovering advancements in healthcare that aren't always taught in schools. If you don't know how to get the results your patients need, start mastering that first. Get a mentor, go to industry events, and get the skills you need to ensure your patients get great outcomes so you don't tarnish your good name and our transformational industry.

Once you have a treatment plan that works, we're ready to start promoting it and changing lives.

Ready? Let's get moving.

Please note: Throughout this book, we share some of our business success stories and the success stories of our doctor clients and members. There are no typical results, and your results may vary based on any number of factors. As with all things, building a strong profitable practice that you enjoy takes consistent effort and self-discipline. Just like staying healthy and fit for life.

CHAPTER 1

WHY THERE'S A TON OF MONEY IN INTEGRATED HEALTHCARE

We've already established there's a major crisis in healthcare in the United States. What we haven't made clear is what that means for you.

As costs rise for patients and chronic diseases like diabetes and heart disease impact a growing number of Americans, the industry is at a crossroads. And while this crisis is sure to get worse before it gets better, make no mistake: the industry is booming.

Millions of consumers are seeking better care than what the current system is offering.

We are at the start of a major shift primarily driven by consumer demand and the frustrated medical leaders who hold the keys to real change.

As today's patients continue to search for new answers to their old healthcare problems, there is plenty of money to be made by those practices that choose to offer something truly different. Just as the winners in the stock market are the ones who can see emerging trends, tomorrow's healthcare winners will be the ones who seize the opportunity to create change in a booming industry with a unique proposition: a movement away from *managed* healthcare towards *transformative* healthcare.

Of course, that means bucking the current system that is supported and upheld by insurance carriers. There's always risk in trying something other than standard adoption—and those with power will continue to fight for their piece of the pie—but the current trends are unsustainable.

Next-level healthcare is the only solution for real change.

That sounds nice, but one of the questions we often get from doctors is, "Can you really build a cash practice and be successful in the industry without insurance contracts?"

There are a lot of misconceptions about people willing to invest in their own health if they have to pay out of their own pockets versus using their insurance.

For decades, we've believed this myth that medical providers have no place asking people for money. We've believed that a doctor who offers supplemental ways for a patient to invest in their health is "greedy" or "pulling one over" on a patient. A doctor who promotes or profits in any form is somehow evil or wrong.

How absurd!

People are desperate for answers and solutions, and in the absence of solutions from their doctor, they're self-diagnosing and experimenting with advice from Instagram, Google, and Netflix!

They're scarfing down purple pills (and worse, the white ones) and we're quietly letting it all happen because we've been taught advertising is only done by hospitals, drug companies, and malpractice attorneys!

Make no mistake. Your ideal patients are looking for and paying for solutions…without you!

IT'S TIME TO CHANGE THE MODEL

The third leading cause of death right now in the United States is medical negligence, according to *The Journal of the American Medical Association*. This is an alarming fact because many medical errors are entirely preventable. Yet many physicians feel trapped by a system that leads to these kinds of results in the interest of safeguarding income through insurance contracts. We've been conditioned to believe that without those contracts, American consumers simply can't or won't pay for their healthcare out of their own pockets.

The truth is, the current insurance industry is conditioning people to pay for a lot of their own medical care. The average individual is paying $4,358 a year for their deductible, and the average family deductible is $7,983.[1] That's money just to manage symptoms and not address the root cause.

I believe it's our job to help patients understand that this money could be put towards care that may actually restore or regenerate their health—if the patient does their part—instead of putting them in the same boat each year and maxing out deductibles.

Think about how many times you have considered quitting the industry, and how many talented doctors you have seen come and go over the years.

Physicians are at a moral crossroads. Dissatisfaction and burnout are at an all-time high.

Dr. John Tait was one of those physicians. I met him eight years ago at a fitness business conference. He was leaving his practice because he felt he could no longer justify being forced to see hundreds of patients a week. He was prescribing only opioids, facilitating only coverup treatments, and in some cases performing procedures that, in the long-term did more harm than good. At the same time, he continued to see decreased reimbursements, red-tape, and insurance denials.

He was at the fitness conference looking to become a personal trainer so he could transform lives another way. I asked him why he didn't just offer these services inside a practice he created. His big reluctance was he had no business and marketing experience.

After some conversation, Dr. Tait took a risk and joined our coaching program. Three years later he won our "Regenerative Practice of the Year" award.

He has a practice full of regenerative, functional, and cash-paying patients—and he's finally doing meaningful work he loves. He let go of the

[1] www.thebalance.com/what-is-the-average-health-insurance-premium-4586358

status quo and all the security it promised and found a new way forward that made all the difference for him, his practice, and the patients he is able to continue serving every day.

IT'S TIME YOU SPEAK UP

More than ever before, people are willing to pay for an outcome they desire because insurance has nothing to offer to solve their problems.

And that's really what we're all hopefully paying for, isn't it? An outcome. We all have problems, we all have the inability to deal with our problems, and we're seeking solutions to immediately and definitively solve them. And as good Americans, we're eager to pull out our wallet and pay for speed or a specific desired outcome—if we can find it.

When you have real health solutions, it's critical you're NOT the best-kept secret in your area.

That is why marketing and sales are the key ingredient in creating a next-level practice. You provide the outcome they are desperately seeking and in return, you earn the impact, income, and independence you deserve.

This great value exchange is about raising both parties' quality of life *without* the unwelcome middlemen of bureaucratic red tape, pharmaceutical influence, and insurance control over what can and can't be offered to your patients.

Marketing and sales do not have to be about sleazy or manipulative tactics. You can learn the methods of selling without selling. This is not about overpromising and underdelivering. It's the opposite: under-promising and overdelivering.

Sharing what you can offer people is about confidently and passionately speaking truth about what it takes for patients to reach the level of health they desire. It's about clearly communicating to prospects how other patients who followed your proven protocol achieved amazing success.

In this short guidebook, I'm going to teach you how to deliver a message that makes you feel great about providing the hope and solutions your prospective patients are searching for.

Your mission, should you choose to accept it, is an opportunity that could propel your business and your personal happiness to the next level and set you on a course of success for the next 10, 20, or 30 years.

People want what integrative and outcome-based healthcare can give them, and they understand they have to pay to get it.

We have a population of people who are:

- In your office for a reason
- Sick and tired of being sick and tired or in pain
- Frustrated
- Looking for answers that no one has figured out
- Looking for a professional who can provide hope
- Looking for a professional who is compassionate
- Looking for someone who listens
- Looking for someone with a good reputation
- Looking for specialists, not generalists
- Looking for alternatives to what they have already tried

They don't want drugs, coverups, or surgery as the first-line treatment. They want safe, minimally invasive, and effective treatment plans that have helped people just like them restore and revitalize their health.

People want health, because health is the greatest wealth, and they will invest their own money to get it.

> *Man. He sacrifices his health in order to make money.*
> *Then he sacrifices money to recuperate his health.*
> *And then he is so anxious about the future that he does not enjoy the present; the result being that he does not live in the present or the future; he lives as if he is never going to die, and then dies having never really lived.*
>
> - Dalai Lama

THIS WORKS ANYWHERE

In the introduction, I mentioned we created the 28,000-square-foot Rejuv Medical in Waite Park, Minnesota. Like most of you, we are surrounded by numerous other medical facilities, with more competition popping up every day.

Despite all that competition and uncertainty regarding insurance coverage, Rejuv is thriving.

The company's total revenue averages just about $8,000,000 a year. Not bad for a mid-size community with plenty of healthcare options.

It's even more exciting to know that the retention rate of patients averages at least three years, and it's climbing with every year of operation.

I won't tell you getting to this level is easy or without investment into skills, knowledge, and a team. You're going to need to grow with your business.

The good news is we have a proven model. We've gone first. We've battled our way through the bureaucracy and taken the arrows in our backs for doing things differently. And now we know how and where to invest to gain traction quickly.

The first skill we need to work on is your ability to reach and inspire people to believe in a new model.

You need to be proficient at marketing and helping people make investments that can change their lives.

How Many New Patients Do You Need?

If you're serious about gaining cash-paying patients, knowing your numbers is essential. In the box below, write the amount of NEW revenue you'd like to ADD to your business this year:

$

Now pick 2-3 different transformation health procedures, programs, or packages you already offer or could confidently offer soon. Choose **services that provide the best outcomes and the greatest joy for you.**

PRODUCTS OR SERVICE YOU COULD MARKET

If they're one-time or short-term services, calculate the total income for the process. If it's a recurring monthly program, calculate the annual value.

Service example: Regenerative Medical Procedure — $6000/patient

Recurring Example: Concierge Health Program — $300/mo. x 12 = $3600

Service ______________________________ $____________/patient

Service ______________________________ $____________/patient

Recurring _______________ $ _____x 12 = $____________/patient

Divide your revenue goal from above by the average of your 2-3 numbers to determine how many new cash-paying patients you need to hit your revenue growth goal.

Revenue Goal	/	Average Annual Value	=	New Patients
$	/	$	=	#

Remember that NEW patients number. It's the target you could reach using the marketing ideas from the rest of this book!

CHAPTER 2

7 REASONS YOU MUST BECOME PROFICIENT AT MARKETING & SALES

We could keep talking about the need to transform our industry, but at this point I want to shift gears and start equipping you to do it. Choosing to offer something different—something truly beneficial to your patients—is going to require that you become great at telling the world what you do and the positive impact it has already had.

In other words, I believe the number one key to success in transformative healthcare is becoming great at marketing and sales.

You can't change lives if you're the best-kept secret in town. You must get good at gaining the attention, trust, and business of others in order to make a difference. To be more specific, here are the top seven reasons to embrace marketing and sales as powerful tools to transform your life and the industry.

1. TO MAKE AN IMPACT AND LEAVE A LEGACY

There are *a lot* of hurting people hoping for a medical solution. Most ordinary people blame circumstances and others for their situation. The government, insurance companies, food manufacturers, and the pharmaceutical industry profit from their confusion and fear.

As a husband and father of four kids, I want to be part of the solution and not a part of the problem. I want to make sure I'm creating a world my family can live and thrive in. By helping redefine our healthcare system, you and I can help make a real, lasting impact.

I believe you chose this profession to change lives and leave a positive mark on future generations too. It's hard to do that when the system is stacked against us.

Doctors are the key to changing healthcare, but so many are frustrated with the current system and feel there is no hope. They don't see how anything will ever change.

The problem is most doctors have never learned how to effectively communicate (market and sell)—which means they have no realistic way to share their new vision of health with their patients and prospects.

I walk into many practices that want to make the move to cash care and offer the non-covered labs and procedures, but the doctors are afraid to discuss alternative options with their existing patients. Patients who already trust them with their health. They can't confidently look them directly in the eye and educate them on their options and what they would do if it were them.

Can you? To make a real impact that lasts, you've got to learn how to reach people and inspire them to take action.

2. TO GET OFF THE HAMSTER WHEEL

At a recent nationally recognized orthopedic conference, I was part of a roundtable of practice executives reviewing the key elements of running a profitable practice. Each group was discussing how many patients their top producing physicians were able to see in a day. One group was cheering that their top physician can see 80 patients a day. Another said 70, and another 60 as if that was a badge of honor. I spoke up:

> "Let's assume that doctor only uses the bathroom once, walks to the next room between each patient, washes their hands after each patient, and somehow spends no time in medical charts. At best he or she has three to four minutes to spend with each patient. I would not want that care for you, a family

> member, or anyone I would refer. We should be ashamed of seeing this as quality care."

This is the reason we have a rising trend of burnout, dissatisfied, and morally conflicted medical providers. That's not to speak of the minimal level of care a patient gets in short 5-minute interactions. Doctors are no longer able to help people the way they desire. It's not your fault, but it is your problem.

If this hamster-wheel level of expectations for you and revolving door care for your clients angers you, too, the world needs you to roll up your sleeves and do something about it.

Unless and until you're proficient at bringing in your own patients on your own terms, you'll always be dependent on the directives and the profit motives of the people above you who measure shareholder profit over value of care.

3. INDEPENDENCE TO HELP PEOPLE BY DOING WHAT'S BEST FOR THE PATIENT

Most owners want the ability to give their patients what they need and want without red tape and bureaucracy. As I wrote in the last chapter, medical negligence is a leading cause of death in the U.S. today, and I believe that's in large part due to the restrictive system that more often puts treatment decisions in the hands of executives and insurance companies than doctors themselves.

Legendary functional medicine physician and pioneer, Joseph Mercola, recently stated this at Mindshare, a healthcare event:

> "Those in control are building the largest tribe and protecting advertisers. It's a threat. PR firms are doing all they can to discredit those that want to heal the world."

We have the science and evidence to not let a diagnosis be the reason for a life of decline. However, we are all fighting a Goliath on steroids. Those in the position of profits over people are doing their best to keep education, research, innovation, and successful outcomes from progressing to be an option for all. They benefit when the coverup treatments and pills continue as the front line of managed healthcare. What motivation do they have to change?

Alternative healthcare providers attempting to educate the public are combating censorship through the news, Google, and social media on topics such as vaccinations, lifestyle medicine, plant medicine, functional medicine, and regenerative medicine. This has led to a confused and confusing public forum on healthcare that does nothing but serve the status quo. This is systemic control and not freedom of choice.

Fighting the system requires marketing and sales skill unlike any time in history. It's not enough to be good at medicine. You've got to be good at overcoming the censorship of those who want to silence you so they can fill their pockets. You've got to share the real, inspiring stories of the patient's lives you have helped change.

4. TO CREATE GREATER INCOME AND RECURRING INCOME

To add insult to injury to you as a doctor, the managed healthcare system places a hard cap on the money you can make via a one-to-one patient care model. Even if you're on a production model, you can only see so many patients.

In transformative healthcare, there are numerous opportunities for you to make money that don't involve your time. We all have seen network marketers with far less education and skills create financial independence selling supplements and online programs while sipping Mai Tais on the beach. Not all, but many, are selling unremarkable solutions. Why can't you succeed with truly transformative services? That alone should get you to wake up and transform your model.

If you start a business and lean into the marketing and sales secrets I'm going to teach you, you can literally write your own destiny. How would you like to provide the opportunity for mission-based providers to work with you while you get a share of what each one of them creates?

You could also provide retail items your patients need that they are currently purchasing elsewhere. Last year we made nearly half a million dollars in supplement sales alone at Rejuv!

That's revenue you're probably letting slip through your fingertips.

Want to keep going? How about the money you're losing charging only for once-and-done visits or procedures? How about another patient leaving and believing there is no hope for them? HealthOvators clients learn how to change the model and create recurring monthly payment models that effectively keep patients committed and engaged.

Best of all, recurring patients reduce your need to constantly refill every hourly slot with new patients.

How would your practice and life change if 40, 50, or 60+ percent of your patients were on a recurring plan?

How would it feel to have month-in, month-out security in predictable income from automatic payment plans and electronic fund withdrawals?

It's these kinds of models our doctors are implementing with remarkable success. Knowing how to define, promote, explain, and communicate_these plans is another reason you want to become proficient at marketing and sales.

Why You Can Charge More Independently

Think about this: if the entire medical system turned around today and added preventative, functional, regenerative, and less-invasive options like nutrition, fitness, health coaching, and energy medicine, would we be prepared to fill the immediate demand? There would be a massive shortage of trained doctors and health and fitness professionals to handle the chronic disease and pain patient population. In addition, the insurance model can only operate with volume buyers due to the rising epidemic of disease and degeneration.

Consumers seeking optimal health are seeking expert health professionals who will slow down long enough to really listen, diagnose, encourage, and work with them to achieve successful outcomes.

To get that level of attention, they'll pay for you to dig deeper with root cause lab analysis, alternative treatments, and greater depth of care.

That's what all this talk about marketing and sales comes down to: successful outcomes. You aren't a door-to-door charlatan selling snake oil. As we have already discussed, the *right* patients will gladly pay for the outcomes you've already helped people just like them achieve. Those outcomes are at the root of your messaging. They're what drive your sales and marketing efforts, and in the end, they are why you can charge more independently.

5. TO ATTRACT THE PEOPLE ALREADY LOOKING FOR WHAT YOU OFFER

Have you searched online for yourself lately? Imagine you or a loved one was faced with a medical condition that your office could correct. They're searching, praying, and hoping for an answer. How hard would it be to find you if they didn't know you or your clinic's name?

People are on the internet looking for natural, safe, minimally invasive, and transformational health solutions. Are you one of the solutions they're finding?

There are millions desperate for answers, and they are looking. Developing your skills in marketing and sales is about being someone they can find and trust. You must learn the words and phrases your preferred patients are typing into search boxes. They are the ones that are actively in search of an expert like you.

Good marketing will get them in the door. Good sales skills will help them say yes to the help they need.

6. TO SERVE MORE MOTIVATED PATIENTS

You may have heard the phrase, "No pay, no pay attention." The more we invest, the more committed we become. Healthcare is no exception.

One of the greatest insights we gained at Rejuv Medical was that the patients who joined our medical fitness facility and/or had a health coach worked harder to improve their life than those who didn't. They were more willing to exchange choices that negatively impacted their health for ones that would help them look and feel the way they desired.

These changes helped them achieve amazing outcomes for injuries, chronic pain, or metabolic syndrome cases. Most of the chief complaints they had were completely resolved after a few months.

Motivated prospective patients buy into your confidence. When you lack confidence in sales and start hedging on the price, discounting, or ignoring the matter, it communicates you may not believe you have the best solution. When you're not convincing, trust is low, and they begin to waffle on their decisions.

Morale and excitement for our model grew exponentially. We had patients accepting responsibility for their health and they were happier and getting significantly better outcomes. It was a win-win scenario.

A big part of the draw for many of my coaching clients to a transformative, integrated healthcare practice is the chance to engage in a true partnership with patients. Marketing and sales are your keys to growing a patient list of cash-care patients, and those patients who are investing personally in their health are the most likely to be fully motivated in seeking positive outcomes with your help.

7. TO GAIN MORE REFERRALS

The final major reason to invest in your own marketing and sales skills can offer an exponential return: referrals. Sure, many healthcare providers operating within the current system enjoy referrals from happy patients. But once you've gotten your practice off the ground and put in the hard work to grow a good patient base of motivated, happy patients, the potential for your practice to continue growing through the power of referrals is tremendous.

Because you change their lives, your patients will become your best walking billboards. Their experiences will do more than any single marketing medium ever could, and every satisfied patient has the potential to bring scores more through your front door. In fact, we have had one patient who has referred *over 100 patients* to us. If that's not worth the hard work of learning to effectively share your value, I don't know what is!

If referrals are not your number one source of new patients, there may be something missing in your outcomes or your ability to communicate your mission and your desire to help more patients just like them.

As you get better at marketing, you'll learn there are all kinds of ways to encourage authentic referrals that fill your waiting list with people predisposed to trust you because of the results they've seen you get for someone else.

CHAPTER 3

THE 7-STEP PROTOCOL TO BECOMING THE INFLUENTIAL DOCTOR WITH A PROFITABLE PRACTICE

Ready to get rolling on your marketing plan? While it'd be ideal to get all the assets you need in place at once, the reality is each item builds on another.

Let's look at the seven-step process we guide our clients through to build the kind of authority and trust necessary to thrive as an independent practice and influential leader.

1. Clear Message
2. Authority Brand
3. Simple Lead Offer
4. Follow-Up Systems
5. Omnipresence
6. Signature Book
7. Keynote Talk

STEP 1: CLARIFY YOUR MESSAGE

There's a big difference between your practice, the hospital, and the clinic down the street. Being able to articulate that difference clearly is critical to your success. Confused consumers don't buy. That's why the first marketing component we work on is clarifying your message.

A common pattern of disconnect I see is that many medical practices and business owners are trying to be everything to everyone. When you do this, there's nothing special about you. That makes it hard to create an emotional connection that inspires people to action.

Income and impact result from having highly specific solutions targeted directly at your ideal patients.

Clear messaging begins with understanding your *ideal* prospects. As they say, "The riches are in the niches." You know what you're best at—and who you can get the best results for—so focus on filling your practice with those people. If there aren't enough, expand your territory. People will travel long distances to get the result they want.

At Rejuv, our target market for our medical fitness program was females age 30 to 55 with an average household income of $100,000+. We knew a lot about that woman. Her behaviors, spending habits, her negative self-talk, and what fears kept her up at night. We also knew what neighborhoods she lived in, what clubs and social communities she congregated in, the ages of her kids, and more.

Having this kind of focus on your target market allows you to develop a message that has direct relevance and appeal by helping solve that specific market's greatest problems.

To that end, the next key to developing a clear message is identifying what you want to be known for. At Rejuv, we believe that we have the top non-surgical, functional, and medical fitness integrated clinics and that we deliver better outcomes than any other practice in the world. Bold claim, I know, but I have yet to see better. Therefore, it is our obligation to market and connect with those in need of and searching for such solutions.

Kaylea Boutwell Lenarz, MD, another HealthOvators client, wanted to be known for pain resolution (not just management) while delivering her message "Power Over Pain" to the world. As you can imagine, there are a lot of patients she can serve from that positioning, but it all starts with her key distinguishing passion: you deserve to live a pain-free life.

What's the one result you want to be the "go-to doctor" for? It should be a service you love to deliver. The thing that you cannot *not* talk about. It gives you energy and enthusiasm to do more of it. It makes you sizzle and shine and gives people an immediate curiosity to want to work with you.

You and your whole team need to know this one result and articulate it clearly in one sentence. Then you need to be sure all your website content and marketing materials reinforce that message clearly and succinctly.

This doesn't mean you don't offer other services, treatments, or procedures. But in order to stand out in a sea of competition, it's critical to first become the go-to expert in one area. Clarify your message to attract prospects to your key offer, and then you can suggest other services as you solve the previous problem. The goal is to continue to optimize and monitor their health to keep them as a patient for life.

Test Your Message

- ❑ Does the name of your practice or business convey the message you want to get across?
- ❑ Does your headline clearly communicate the transformation or typical outcome you deliver, and is it using the words that most of your patients use when describing what they want?
- ❑ Are you and your team able to clearly communicate what you offer in 30 seconds or less and have people ask you to tell them more?
- ❑ Are you using language that your target audience understands and speaking at a junior-high level for full comprehension?
- ❑ Do the majority of people who land on your webpage stay longer than one minute?

If you can't check every box above, it's time to put some hard work into developing a compelling message that's consistent across the board.

STEP 2: DEVELOP YOUR AUTHORITY

Once we have a clear message, we can start bringing the whole brand into alignment. Your brand includes your message, story, logo, clothes, pictures, energy, health, verbal and non-verbal communication, office ambiance, team culture, pricing, messaging, intake, treatment plans, and every other element that makes up a patient or prospect's perception of who you are.

Let's discuss the three most important matters of creating authority: first impressions, your story, and your unique protocol.

Manage First Impressions

If you want to be regarded as the best in your region or as a thought leader, you have to be perceived that way by your market. A good brand analysis looks at your marketing and your messaging from an outside perspective and ensures that everything is reinforcing the way you want to be seen, heard, and experienced.

There's a lot we could go into here, but I suggest you start with a basic review of your website, print materials, lobby, front desk, and the visual experience of a patient on their walk back from the waiting room. Do any aspects of these materials or spaces conflict with the key message you're working to communicate? Make a list of 5-10 items you could delegate to someone to clean up or update—and give them authority to get it done.

Encourage your team to start living your brand and embodying what you stand for as the leading center you want to be.

Brand Disconnects I Often Observe

- ☒ A regenerative medicine clinic offering $10,000 stem cell packages—with cluttered front desks and dirty exam rooms.
- ☒ A weight loss clinic with candy at the front desk and at trade show booths.
- ☒ Doctors selling functional medicine and transformative health programs while remaining very unhealthy themselves.
- ☒ Doctors offering a cash service to a patient without communicating with verbal and non-verbal certainty that this is the best step for the patient, or that if they were in a similar situation, they would be doing the same for themselves.
- ☒ Selling high ticket programs with cheap logos and without high-quality literature and marketing materials.
- ☒ Asking each team member to explain what it is that the clinic offers—and getting a different answer from everyone.

Tell Stories: Yours and Your Patients

The next step is to create your brand story. When we start telling our story of why we do what we do and what that means for our prospects, we can start to connect with them in a genuine way. People do not just buy on facts and logic—they want an emotional connection. They want to know why you do what you do because it shows that you care beyond money. They also want to hear the success stories of your patients, to hear how you do what you do and why it works.

An Influential Doctor must become a great storyteller because facts tell…but stories sell.

First, you'll want to work on your back story. Most physicians do not tell their personal stories and reasons for doing what they do. Starting now, you do. Review your life's journey and find the pivotal moments, experiences, and decisions that led you to where you are today. Then find ways to share your story with your prospects. Let them connect and relate to you and your mission.

Your personal stories should be relatable. This is what will attract people and allow them to connect with your mission, and they will work better than any other marketing factor. Be authentic and a little vulnerable in your stories. Use them to build trust, authority, and connection.

Next, you want to start collecting a lot of patient success stories. It's one thing to say you're great at what you do. Prospects want to see evidence, and that's why you need a lot of patient case studies and testimonials. Start collecting them. Assign your staff to help. Then start looking for ways to incorporate them into all your marketing, from your website to the waiting room material. Build trust, calm fears, and overcome disbelief by constantly putting success stories in front of your audience.

Brand Your Unique Protocol

This is one of the biggest game-changers for any clinic, and one of the most exciting things we work on with our clients: branding your unique protocol.

You may have heard the phrase, "Whoever names it claims it." At this point in cash medicine, we are past the phase where true pioneers were looked upon as completely insane, quacks, or putting the world at risk for practicing medicine that was outside the box of traditional managed care.

At the same time, simply marketing functional, regenerative, preventative, or transformative health is not enough anymore. There is competition everywhere now, and using words like "preventative" won't be enough to stand out. However, creating a named process that is clear to the outcome you provide—and showing the market you do it differently and consistently in a way they understand—is another story.

Sharing Success Stories

However, someone finds you, their next phase in exploring what you have to offer will be to search through your reviews and success stories.

Each story you make available is an opportunity to relate with your prospects' greatest challenges and potential objections to your services while offering them a glimpse of what it looks like to come through to the other side with your help.

While we never tell patients what to say in their testimonials, we do use these five questions to help them write a short letter or record a short video, both of which are valuable:

Testimonial Questions:

1. What was the number one reason that nearly prevented you from coming to __?
2. What was your life like prior to being seen by us at ____?
3. Tell me about your experience and treatment here.
4. What was your transformation with our medical center?
5. What would you tell someone who was on the fence about coming to ____?

Make it a weekly goal to get 1-2 testimonials for every service you offer and every objection there may be to that service.

At Katalyst Pain Management and Restorative Treatment Center in Missouri, we worked to brand Dr. Kaylea Boutwell Lenarz's message as "Power Over Pain," made possible through her unique protocol "Pain Resolution Plan." We identified and named three key phases of the patient journey: Rethink, Rebuild, and Regenerate. Under each, we list key services so patients can see the logical progression they need to follow in order to better manage or reverse their chronic pain.

Having your patient journey mapped out builds trust and confidence. Of course, not every patient starts at the same point, and some may not go through every step. But having the full map not only makes it easier to market it, but also to explain why a patient may not be getting the results they wanted when they try to skip portions of the preferred treatment protocol.

So, to summarize Step 2: Building Your Authority, we complete three key items: improve first impressions, create compelling stories, and brand the journey.

See how incredibly valuable these key details could be for your practice? No one else will have the same identical offerings or message you do even though you may offer the same services that many other practices do.

Now we're ready to really capture your market and start pulling in better leads.

STEP 3: CREATE A SIMPLE LEAD OFFER

Let's talk briefly about the fundamentals of advertising now. Most small businesses are wasting a lot of money trying to stay top-of-mind with everyone everywhere so that they'll (hopefully) buy from them when the time is right. Coca-Cola can afford to play that game. And a hospital. That's fine for their deep pockets. We're going to be much more selective and intentional with your advertising budget.

I want you to apply the tenets of direct response marketing instead. Direct response advertisements include an offer in every ad, printed item, and web page. You can even make an offer on a billboard! The offer simply invites good prospects to sign up (or "opt-in") via email or physical mailing address to gain access to specific information sent *directly* for them.

This form of marketing is extremely valuable because it allows you to capture an interested prospect's contact information so you can continue to market to (think educate, prequalify, and presell) them *at a much lower cost* than you'd pay to keep trying to reach and remind them via regular ads. It also gives you crucial time to build trust and a relationship using the messaging and stories we developed in steps one and two.

To take advantage of direct response marketing, you need a few simple lead offers, like:

- A quiz or self-assessment
- A short training series or challenge
- A live information session or webinar
- An introductory or trial offer
- A journal or tracking sheet
- A checklist of all your favorite health and wellness solutions
- Recipes, grocery list, workouts, or sample routines
- A summary of 3-7 health principals to incorporate on their own
- A summary of your unique branded protocol, a/k/a "patient journey"

You might have one or two of the items above already sitting on your computer. We have several of them already done for our HealthOvators clients to use as theirs. These offers aren't terribly time-intensive to create, and yet they provide immediate value to anybody remotely interested in your services—wherever they happen to encounter your message.

A Protocol Book Lead Offer

One of the most effective strategies we're adopting for our doctors is what our publishing partner Niche Pressworks calls a "Protocol Book." In fact, you're reading mine now. Nicole Gebhardt, the CEO, helped me extract this book idea out of my longer bestselling book *Cash Practice Success.* I'm sure you can imagine that a lot more doctors will be willing and able to read this book cover-to-cover than they will my 250-page book.

A Protocol Book is a short, easy-to-read book that explains who you are, what you do, and why you do it. It's typically specific to one product or service, so you might end up having several on niche topics.

Because it's a real book, people value it more than they would a brochure or email series. Because it's a *short* book (under 100 pages), **statistics show 60% of prospects will read it cover to cover...usually in the comfort of their favorite chair!**

Protocol books are different from the long hardcover books most doctors want to write, which we refer to as "Signature Books." We'll talk about those in Step 6. Protocol books are intentionally short for readership, inexpensive to print, and written to inspire prospects to request one-on-one help.

Think about the remarkable implications of having your ideal prospects spending 45 minutes reading your marketing message, learning about what you do and why...before they come for their initial visit! A protocol book pre-qualifies and presells for you so that you can get right to the specifics of a treatment plan in an initial visit.

One good protocol book in your marketing arsenal is a marketing and sales game-changer!

A Protocol Book checks off all the key marketing requirements, which is what makes it so valuable:

- ✓ Your story
- ✓ Authority brand positioning ("We published a book about that...")
- ✓ Client stories and testimonials
- ✓ Your protocol explained
- ✓ An (extremely) attractive lead offer
- ✓ Easy to give away
- ✓ Easy to consume and understand

Best of all, people keep and share helpful books with others. We recommend you give at least two to every one of your patients so they have one to keep and one to give away to a friend who needs you (because that's what you'll ask them to do).

Interested in creating your Protocol Book? You'll find Niche Pressworks' contact information in the back of this book.

STEP 4: IMPLEMENT RELIABLE FOLLOW-UP SYSTEMS

We're all busy, and people get distracted. Statistics say it takes 8-15 message touches for most people to take action on an ad or offer. We've already established why you will want to move from traditional advertising to direct response marketing so that you can build a list of prospects. Your follow-up system is how you'll turn your prospects—from simple lead offers, speaking engagements, referrals, or even first-time office visits that don't convert—into patients.

When I say the word "system", it means you have a process that's documented, scripted, and consistent. Thankfully there's great technology to take care of most of this for you. We help our doctors set up these systems using a Customer Relationship Management (CRM) tool like Ontraport or Keep (formerly Infusionsoft).

For new leads, we follow a proven, advanced sequence using a mix of case studies, testimonials, and offers to educate while addressing their main fear and objections. A good CRM will not only send emails to your candidates, but it can also send trigger notices to specific members of your team reminding them to call, write a note, send a package, or whatever might be appropriate for the stage a lead is in.

Follow-up sequences for existing or past patients typically include information and invitations based on their journey progress. For you, it's a chance to sell new services that will continue to help them obtain better outcomes. For the patient, it's custom content just for them—and that goes a long way.

It's extremely liberating to have these systems in place and know you've got automated tools following up with your leads while you sleep. Even if your team forgets, the system won't.

Should You Hire a Sales Specialist?

By far, the biggest difference maker for both cash and insurance-based sales for us at Rejuv Medical was hiring a Regenerative Specialist/Patient Advocate/Case Manager whose primary role was talking to all our leads and following up with existing and past patients.

Our first hire was Rob O., who had recently graduated as an LPN. He was a college roommate of mine, and he had used car sales experience. I recruited him when I saw how a trained sales professional could make a huge difference in our practice. The decision paid off. Now hiring and training a good sales specialist is one of the first hires we add to any cash practice. Most medical professionals struggle with sales, so most practices, save for some dentist and chiropractic offices, have next to no follow-up.

I know that even at this point the word "sales" may conjure negative associations in your mind. But never have we asked our team to make false promises, oversell, hard-sell, or haggle a patient in any way. There is a way to do this with complete integrity that your patients will appreciate. Our salesperson is following up on care a prospect is already interested in. This follow-up demonstrates we care. We use scripts and defined boundaries to ensure we keep the highest reputation.

STEP 5: DEVELOP OMNIPRESENCE

The first four steps are your foundation. With those in place, you can confidently market and ensure a better return on your efforts.

The next step to becoming an Influential Doctor (and a profitable one, at that) is learning how to create one piece of content and disseminate it to multiple platforms so you're leveraging your time and reaching a lot more people.

Let's use video as an example. Suppose you and I made a list of ten frequently asked questions from your patients and prospects. Now, imagine you blocked an hour and recorded each question and answer in a separate 2-4-minute video and gave each a great title that's optimized for Google.

Every video would reinforce your key message (from Step 1) and end with you telling your listener to sign up for one of your simple lead offers (Step 3) to get more information. You'd quickly have a library of 10 short videos addressing the most pressing questions on your topic!

The goal of omnipresence is to build your authority brand and celebrity status by getting seen, found, heard, read, and discovered on multiple channels.

You could feature one video a week for the next ten weeks and schedule each one to go out on YouTube, Facebook, Instagram, LinkedIn, Twitter,_TikTok, email, etc. You could have them transcribed and cleaned up as optimized articles to feature on your blog or in email. You could then have that written content repurposed for another lead offer or book.

Doing this with FAQs is just one idea. You can do the same thing with team member introductions, facility tours, procedure details, patient interviews, peer interviews, etc. The ideas are endless. I bet you could create a list of 52 (weekly) ideas in one sitting.

All of these messages being disseminated in multiple ways pay off by helping more people get to know, like, and trust you as an authority in your space…and that's how you start transforming the industry and creating real impact and income.

STEP 6: CREATE YOUR SIGNATURE BOOK

With your brand message clearly defined and your marketing and follow-up systems in place, you're starting to get remarkable traction in the industry as a whole. This is the time we help you take your message to the next level with a "Signature Book."

We already mentioned in Step 3 that the first book for any doctor with a physical practice should be a Protocol Book. That'll help you fill your office with ideal patients. It's also faster and easier to write than a longer book.

A Signature Book is a status move at a whole new level. This is the marketing step that'll help you get national (or even international) paid speaking engagements and media attention (TV, magazine, radio, podcasts), especially when we do the work to earn you #1 bestselling author status.

My bestselling Signature Book is *Cash Practice Success: How to See Half the Patients, Increase Your Income, Eliminate Insurance and Practice Medicine that Restores and Regenerates Health* (available on Amazon).

Publishing that bestseller in 2018 earned me the opportunity to speak on major stages like Club Industry, SUCCEED, AAOE, AAOM, MFN, MFA, FAI, and IDEA. I used that book, along with all the other six steps in this process, to co-found MedFit, launch HealthOvators, and become a thought leader in our industry.

Inside *Cash Practice Success,* I outline my full Unique Branded Protocol: "The 5 Pillars of Practice Success". (This Protocol Book you're reading right now focuses on Pillar 3: Marketing and Sales.)

Your Signature Book will build on your practice success and take your message to a larger audience.

When it comes to defining the right strategy for your Signature Book and Protocol Book(s), you need Nicole Gebhardt at Niche Pressworks.

Writing a book (or having one written for you) is a big investment into your business and brand. After seeing a lot of people flop with their books, we've chosen to partner with Nicole's team to help our doctors do theirs right the first time.

There's a difference between *any* book and the *right* book, and that's their specialty. You don't want a one-star book representing your brand on Amazon. They will help you plan, write (or ghostwrite), publish, and promote the right bestseller for your authority brand. They also can help you improve and republish a book that's underperforming.

STEP 7: CREATE YOUR KEYNOTE TALK AND MEDIA MATERIAL

Once you have a strong Signature Book, the next step is to convert that message into your keynote presentation and media material for a publicist to promote.

The goal is to help you make a greater impact by earning more paid speaking and free media. We suggest you create your Signature Book before your keynote because it'll help you acquire better speaking engagements—and you'll have something to sell in the back of the room. The process of writing your book will also help you organize your thoughts and strengthen your message.

Keep in mind that your Keynote and your Signature Book are speaking to a much broader audience than patients in your local market. On your journey to becoming an Influential Doctor, you will be asked to present on numerous talks. Each time you engage with a new host or event, you'll have a slightly different audience with their own unique needs or desires. Your job is to combine their objectives with your key messages.

For example, let's say a physician going through this process has a deep passion for weight loss programs as a means to address the root causes of diseases like diabetes and heart disease. Their key message might take on slightly different shapes depending on the audience:

- **When speaking to the American Heart Association,** they might focus a little more closely on the long-term effects of their weight loss approach on heart health.

- **When doing a podcast popular among people with diabetes,** their message may have less to do with heart disease and more to do with the importance of long-term lifestyle change as a key to lowering or eliminating dependence on insulin.
- **When appearing on a national morning show,** they may focus on offering unique and practical insights into how people can change their lives with a customized approach to diet and exercise.

The services you would offer a prospect in any of these audiences may ultimately be the same or very similar, but what matters is your ability to be flexible with your message, so it focuses on the outcomes most important to each audience.

The ability to continuously improve your communication skills is your greatest opportunity to continue to grow your impact and income. This will be true for keynotes, video content, webinars, office visits, team meetings, networking opportunities, and with vendors. This is the one area I recommend you seek to self-evaluate and also have experienced professionals evaluate how you performed each chance you get.

Here are some of the most important disciplines you'll work on as we develop your keynote opportunities and media material:

- ❑ **Compelling, attention-getting titles:** topics that earn the mic and fill the room
- ❑ **Bold promises:** a clear return on the investment of the audience's time
- ❑ **Connection:** the ability to provide an emotional experience for the audience
- ❑ **Clarity:** the right mix of good stories, content, and slides to deliver a message without overwhelming the listeners
- ❑ **Clear objectives:** understanding the goals of the host and audience
- ❑ **Informative entertainment**: knowing how to hold the audience's attention and keep them engaged
- ❑ **Quality**: professional technology, tone, audiovisuals, pace, and timing

- ❑ **Practice:** rehearsing material and planning for the unplanned
- ❑ **Compelling calls-to-action:** converting listeners into leads

THE NEXT STEP: ALWAYS IMPROVING

These seven steps represent an enormous transformation. It might sound like a lot reading through them all so quickly right now—and make no mistake that it's a lot of work—but taken one step at a time, this process has proven itself time and time again. And just as this process is designed to continually improve your abilities as a communicator, it also works because it's focused on continually improving *itself*.

Arriving at the end of Step 7 with a truly engaging keynote isn't the end of the journey, but simply an opportunity to then take a step back and level-up every component of your messaging machine.

Maybe you'll find as you begin your national speaking tour that patients at your practice are continuing to ask at the end of their first office visit if your services are covered by insurance. That doesn't mean you're reaching the wrong patients, necessarily, but it does mean you have work to do in further refining your message. You'll ask, where along the way—from your website, to the messaging your staff uses, to the materials you offer about your services—can you do a better job of educating prospects about how you are different and why that could be so good for them, it's worth paying out of pocket?

From this point forward, your main focus is investing your time wisely so that you can continue to sell without selling. It's about constantly improving what works, cutting out what doesn't, and learning to convert even more of your prospects into long-term patients so you can transform their lives.

Improving Your Speaking Skills

One of the biggest breakthroughs I've ever had was when I attended a high-ticket speaker training event. At this event, you had two attempts to give a presentation. I was good on my first run but had lots of feedback for improvement. I took the feedback, adjusted my talk and, over the next day and a half, I practiced continuously. I spoke for the second time and nailed all but one part.

My first reaction was, 'I messed up.' I was unhappy with my performance because I had done better in the previous practice runs. The coach wondered why I was being so hard on myself, and I explained that I have very high expectations for myself. He asked me, "But when you work hard, do you grow?" I said, "Yes." Then he asked if I'm committed to practicing, and I of course told him I was.

"So then stop this negative pressure you put on yourself and focus on measuring your progress!" the coach exclaimed.

My mindset immediately changed. I started developing a love for the *process* and focused less on being perfect. I no longer beat myself up—I just measure my progress. If I am lacking progress, I simply ask myself if I am doing the work necessary to improve. If I am doing the work, I know I will naturally get better in time.

Becoming an excellent communicator is an area that I feel is very important for all of us to grow in to have influence and authority in redefining healthcare. Many of us grow to be confident in one-on-one communication. I know most of you have the ability to cover all the main elements of connecting, evaluating, prescribing, and treating with your patients. This is the same thing but in front of more people. Show your heart, passion to help and your skills for changing lives and remember that, like all things in life, getting better at public speaking isn't about the destination—it's about the journey.

CHAPTER 4

WHAT'S HOLDING YOU BACK?

Before we go any further, we need to address the elephant in the room. If having a cash practice is so great, why aren't more doctors dumping insurance and doing it? There are a few common hurdles that come with running your own practice, no matter the business model. And while the prospect of starting and growing a truly independent practice might seem like a huge task, in my experience, there are really just two major factors that hold physicians like you back.

Let's explore both of them now.

FACTOR #1: YOU THINK YOU HAVE TO FIGURE IT ALL OUT ALONE

I'm going to put this in plain language: **you do not have to figure this all out alone.** Starting a business from scratch is an overwhelming prospect, but the help we can offer you through HealthOvators is a far cry from starting from scratch.

The first aspect of this is understanding how valuable it is to have an experienced coach. Someone who can help you sort out what works and what doesn't. Someone who can save you from making costly errors and losing valuable time.

You need a mentor who has done *exactly* what you want to do so you model their success. It's that simple.

"If you want to go fast, go alone; if you want to go far, go together." - African Proverb

The second risk of "figuring it out all alone" is isolation. I meet doctors all the time who are exhausted and painted into a lonely corner because they've bought into a belief that they've got to do it all. There's no support community, no team, no structure, and no system for ensuring things get done.

Having a team allows you to stay focused on what matters most while keeping you out of the day-to-day grind of your business. You can't work ON your business if you're constantly working IN your business. Doing your charts, bookkeeping, administrative tasks, routine procedures, meeting with patients, and even house chores…all while still trying to be a good partner, mother, father, and friend. There's just not enough of you to go around.

Having a community means you're among a group of peers who understand you, can empathize with what you're going through and know how to build structure around your unique talents.

Working in isolation means that you have no one to talk about what I like to call the "next level truth" about business and life.

I spend many behind-the-scenes hours with doctors who are dealing with real challenges like guilt from spouses who feel neglected; disappointment over launches that only yielded a handful of patients; fears about cash flow from a fledgling startup; and overwhelm from having to carry the weight of a business, patients, and a family who all expect you to be a superhero.

We all need a place where we can feel safe to talk about the next level truths about running a business, whether it's the 5% that's going well or the 5% that's not going so well.

I'm not immune to this either. I have coaches and communities I pay to be a member of, and so should you. We need to surround ourselves with successful practice and business owners and model their systems and habits.

Not only is it the wisdom of my mentors that has been my biggest difference maker, it's also being in the room with others, friends who are also looking to grow and break mental chains that keep many shackled for life. It takes a community to do this work. You need to be in an environment where people are positive, where they support you, where they get the next-level stuff, and are able to really truly empathize with you.

When you share that you just got your first cash-paying patient, or just made $10,000 dollars, or got published in the *New York Times*, or scored $30,000 in revenue from your keynote talk, your community will understand and celebrate with you. Their genuine excitement raises your confidence and brings the whole group up to the next level.

FACTOR #2: YOU THINK IT'S ABOUT YOU

Once you've come to terms with the fact that you'll need help to succeed in this industry, the next major obstacle to clear hits a little closer to home. You need to understand that this is not about you.

Maybe you don't feel qualified to branch out on your own, so you keep dosing out prescriptions and ignoring your inner plea to find a better way. Maybe you're intimidated at the prospect of being a leader or afraid of how people will see you. All these fears and limiting beliefs result from what I call "me thinking."

You need to shift your thinking and start believing in the mission you have to change lives and make a real impact.

I get it. If you would have told me when I was a fitness trainer at Gold's Gym, that I would be coaching doctors around the world on building million-dollar practices…I would have told you you're nuts. But step-by-step, I learned, applied, and did it. If I can do it, I *know* you can do it.

You are one of a kind. When you show up and share your story, experience, passion, and convictions, it matters.

If you see inadequate care rampant in your network or know that your ideal patients are headed to the slacker down the street when they should be coming to you…take a look in the mirror and ask yourself why you're letting it happen.

This is about your patient, about your family, about humanity, and about you living your truth.

Many amazing medical professionals let self-doubt stand between them and the fortunes that they deserve and the impact to be had. It's not that there's some hidden force out there preventing us from achieving what we're destined to achieve. All that's holding us back lies between our ears.

That's where there is a little voice saying that we're not enough:

> *"Somebody else is already doing this."*
> *"They're so much more gifted than me."*
> *"If I put myself out there, I may look or sound bad."*
> *"What will people think about me?"*
> *"Who am I to say that I can help someone else?"*

We have all fallen victim to it at times. We've spent our lives waiting for someone to tell us we are worthy.

"Surely I can't call myself a medical thought leader because no one has given me permission."

Sam Horn, author of *POP!,* says, "Name it, Claim it, Fame it!" Very little right now is completely new. But you and your story are unique. The exact way you approach your protocol and how you name it is unique.

This is what thought leaders do. They take time to communicate how they are different. That's all you need to do and then let the results speak for themselves. (Well, actually, we'll be sure to market those stories too!)

Learning to Focus on Your Mission, Not Yourself

I barely graduated high school. If I wasn't good at sports, there was no way they would have let me pass due to my behavior and my tell-it-as-I-saw-it attitude. I never really applied myself within any high-school curriculum in English, math, or science. I technically shouldn't even have received a high school diploma. I just got lucky that I did just enough to not get fully kicked out so I could play.

After graduation, I built water towers with my father and the business he worked for because there was no way I was going to get into a university. I learned what hard work was and I missed out on partying and baseball. I had to go to community college and take one year of prerequisites before I could even get a college credit.

Once I realized that getting a college education was *my* choice, I started to like it. I realized I wasn't dumb. I applied myself and was awarded Academic All-American in the sport of baseball. I finished grad school with a 3.97 GPA and was so mad one professor gave me an A- and I couldn't talk my way to a 4.0 despite my best attempts. (I bet I could now.)

The point of my story is we are capable of *anything* we put our energy, focus, and passion into. I wanted to work in professional sports originally, but I fell in love with helping people as a personal trainer. I had no medical background when I joined Rejuv, but I saw an opportunity to introduce integrated fitness into healthcare…and then I just kept learning, applying, and putting myself out there even when it was uncomfortable.

So, if you're looking inside and questioning whether you really know something that nobody else in healthcare does, stop. That's not the question you need to be asking.

Ask if you have something of value to add to the health community. If you do, it's your responsibility to do it.

If you can get a patient the outcomes faster than they can get on their own or at another practice, then that's all you need. That's all that patient cares about. They don't care where you went to school or what kind of letters are after your name. I know that makes you feel proud, and it should. You worked hard. But that does nothing for your patients.

And who cares about what the rest of the world thinks? The rest of the world is not paying you. You are not marketing to your peers. You need to connect with the person looking for a solution they haven't been able to find before you.

The Impact You're Having

The following is a letter I received from Dr. Vilen, a colleague of mine at Rejuv Medical. It arrived on my last day as I sold out of the two companies I helped co-found so I could focus solely on my one goal of helping frustrated doctors worldwide attract and convert cash care patients.

It not only touched my heart; it should also show you what's possible when you get out of your own way and believe in your mission.

> *JR,*
>
> *Sorry on the delay of getting this to you. I had wanted to get this to you Friday but was up and down with emotions. I do think it's best you are moving on as your skills can change the world. I know you will do great things as everyone has told you. You will reach so many lives on your new venture. You have a special gift working with doctors.*
>
> *I'm not sure I have told you this before. We are not an easy breed to work with on so many levels (as you know) but you have the ability to connect with doctors on a completely different level than any other mentor I have had before. Joel taught me new technical skills to be able to use and for that I will be forever grateful. You taught me something no one else has been able to before and I will forever be in debt to you for that. You gave me confidence, self-esteem and a different view of presenting transformation to patients, other doctors and healthcare workers.*
>
> *You will change healthcare (you are-we all are) and you will on a grand level, and you may not even know how far your impact reaches. Each doctor you talk to (I know it from working with you, have heard, and seen) you make a unique connection that brings out a need and want to grow to be better. Not just doing more stem cells and making more money, but the realization that this is the best way to take care of patients, and the more you do, the more you make, the more things you can do to help the patients. Great*

results keep more patients coming, and make other doctors interested.

Every doctor you talk to takes that and goes back to each patient with this newfound confidence in their treatments, counseling, education and their willingness to try something new and tell others. Both Erik and I are examples of what you can do to develop someone. Way beyond marketing, sales and business. It's not just you being an empath or all the hours you have put in, or your work ethic. It's something special you have to connect with others, and teach them to connect with others. I don't know exactly what it is, and we don't need to know, but use it.

Videos, podcasts, talks on stages are all great ways of getting out there, but independent consulting one-on-one, small groups, reading individuals and their needs and communicating this to them is your gift. More people hear you in the large forums, but more patients are reached by better medicine and better healthcare, with you going to their practice to make it better and make it what it needs to be.

I'm happy you have been able to get the training and have done the work to make this next step possible for you. You deserve so much recognition. Know both Erik and I appreciate you and can never thank you enough for what you have done for us. And shown us.

Thank you. If we can do anything for you to help. Please let us know.

— Jana, Erik and family

Once I learned how to market and then sell one-on-one, and I saw how our programs were getting results for patients they couldn't get on their own or elsewhere, I made it my *mission* to help as many people as possible get the life they desired with transformational health and regenerative medicine.

It was no longer about me; it was about *you* and the others like you I know I can help. That message and mission makes me feel unstoppable, even though I still have my own insecurities!

When you stretch yourself and take massive, albeit imperfect, action it's because you have courage, you have the right mindset and your thinking more about who you can help than yourself. When you have the right mindset, you integrate tools to get past the fear and into action. When you have the right mindset, you ask for help so you can take fast action and stop worrying about whether it's perfect or not.

When you have the right mindset, what used to seem impossible becomes possible because you start to push past the fear knowing that *feeling the fear* is all part of the process.

Maybe now you're thinking I'm saying that a single mindset shift is all it takes to be successful. Of course not. Making a 7-figure-plus, life-changing practice—or even an extra $5K or $10K a month—doesn't happen overnight without you doing the inner and outer work. Yet it is possible for you.

Find the support you need to follow the practices that work, stay focused on your mission of truly helping the patients you'll reach, and *nothing* can hold you back.

CHAPTER 5

HOW TO IDENTIFY YOUR IDEAL PATIENTS

At this point, we've covered a lot of ground. We've discussed why now is the time to build a profitable, independent healthcare practice. We've broken down why marketing and sales are critical tools in that endeavor, explored the steps you'll take towards becoming The Influential Doctor, and even addressed some of what might be holding you back.

The next key is identifying exactly who your ideal patients really are. The best patients for transformative cash practices are focused on outcomes, willing to try new things if they believe they'll bring results, and ready to put in the hard work to change.

But how do you find people who fit that bill in your market?

There's a BIG difference between people who NEED your services and people who WANT your services.

It's a pretty safe bet that every single adult over 40 has heard that they need to eat healthy foods and exercise regularly. The reality is that the vast majority willfully *don't.*

And yet, so many health professionals will waste thousands of dollars trying to convince those not ready or searching that they should live a healthier life.

Why start at ground zero?

You'll get much faster results marketing to people already interested in obtaining a specific goal—and that takes some real skill.

GETTING FOUND THROUGH SEO

Marketing to this audience is all about branding to attract their attention and then connecting with them at the right time in their life. It probably won't be an emergency situation. That ideal patient who is truly ready for change has probably been dealing with their symptoms, diagnosis, or pain for quite some time. They are skeptical that anything will work for them—but that doesn't mean they aren't looking for relief.

Making sure they find you is all about being marketing savvy, including important tactics like search engine optimization (SEO). With the right help from an experienced SEO firm, and a solid understanding of *who* your ideal patient is, you can optimize your website to appeal to those people who are most likely to become your patients. When you understand the phrases your ideal patients are using to find the outcomes they want, you can work to put your message in front of them when they're already in search mode.

I saw the power of this firsthand as I built Rejuv Medical using the very principles I'm teaching you here. We didn't become one of the top-volume stem cell clinics in the world on our own, or by accident. We made it a priority to invest in SEO and produce content with keywords we knew our ideal patients were already using. Then, using what we learned about those keywords, we were able to build paid advertising strategies that wouldn't waste money on people who weren't self-identifying as prospects with real potential.

FINDING EFFECTIVE MOMENTS TO CAPTURE ATTENTION OFFLINE

Your digital presence isn't your only opportunity to get your message in front of those motivated seekers you want to reach. Learning to capture the attention of your ideal patients offline is in many ways very similar to capturing their attention online. Rather than identifying keywords they're likely to use, you identify times when they'll be most likely to be thinking seriously about their health—and most likely to pay for better health themselves.

When are those times?

- When they're already focused on making healthy choices, like when they attend a health fair, shop at a farmer's market, or go to Whole Foods, etc.
- When they're thinking about being physically active, such as at a walk-for-the-cure event, an athletic shoe or sporting goods store, a golf course, a tennis club, or while planning a big vacation
- When they're in the waiting room for a doctor or physical therapy appointment at another practice (imagine having your Protocol Book in those lobbies)
- When they're focused on self-care or their looks, and already engaging with a dermatologist, dentist, massage therapist, hair salon, etc.
- When a friend or loved one is diagnosed with a serious health condition—or they personally experience an alarming event or scary doctor's report
- When their friend (who happens to be your patient) is celebrating a milestone or good news report that gets their attention
- Or even simply by targeting direct mail campaigns to affluent neighborhoods—indicating they'll be able to pay for your services

The bottom line: it's easier, faster, and less expensive to convert a prospect into a patient when they're already interested in the message you have to offer.

But what are the most effective marketing tactics to meet seekers where they are in those moments when they're most likely to engage you? That's what we need to discuss next…

CHAPTER 6

HOW TO GET PATIENTS FAST

Now you know WHAT to say—or at least how to go about developing your key message.

You know WHO to say it to and how you can find those seekers that will make the best clients for your practice.

You've even been empowered to know WHEN it makes sense to share your message (and when it's mostly a waste of your time and money).

Let's get to the nitty-gritty: WHERE to say it.

ONLINE VS. OFFLINE MARKETING

As I suggested in the previous chapter, marketing is more effective when you mix both online and offline tactics. **But with integrated healthcare, you've got to think offline a lot more than many other types of businesses might.**

There are many people that will NEVER create a Social Media account or sign up for an email marketing list.

Yes, I said NEVER. A lot of high-wealth professionals and Boomers are stubborn that way. But that doesn't mean they aren't active in their community, affluent, or well connected. The best strategy is to reach them offline, and then follow up your efforts online.

That said, let's start with online strategies since that's what you are probably most familiar with, and we can cover it quickly.

OUR MOST EFFECTIVE ONLINE MARKETING

For the purposes of this book, we'll define "online" as digital marketing through a screen. This world can be complex and require a lot of split testing to learn which tactics work best for your brand, but in my experience, there are three primary winners.

This may feel a little redundant to what we've discussed before…but they're worth repeating in this context.

Create a Compelling Simple Lead Offer

The first tactic won't do anything by itself but is the fuel that drives the other two: developing a simple lead offer. The "offer" part of this concept is *content.* This is a short report—maybe it's a PDF download or a gated page of your website—that explains your unique protocol and shows prospects the kinds of results you can bring them.

We covered that in Step 3 of your marketing strategy earlier.

Your simple lead offer needs to be quick, approachable, and, most of all, *free*. It offers a little bit of insight into a potential new solution to the problem that has been plaguing your prospective patient. The offer works as the carrot that will encourage people to sign up for more information.

Build an Email List of Prospects

Email marketing is priceless because it allows you to stay connected and keep building a relationship until a prospect is ready to say, "Yes!" to your invitation. **To get patients fast, you need to make it your #1 priority to build an email list of good prospects as quickly as you can.**

Start by going through every local connection you already have and reach out to them with a single, personal email invitation. Don't spam people, and never put someone on your bulk mailing list without their permission.

Just reach out individually to each contact and tell them what you specialize in. Then, ask them if they'd like to be included on your mailing list to receive great health information that they can't get from most doctors.

As you build your email list, you'll want and need to stay in contact with them regularly. That can get difficult when you consider all the other things you need to be doing, so we recommend that you mail once a week. Remember: it could be a quick letter or one of your short FAQ videos. It doesn't have to be a complicated message, just a genuine one.

Run Ads

When it comes to reaching the vast majority of ideal patients, Facebook and Instagram are definitely the social media channels of choice. They're there more than any other online channels.

Most adults have a Facebook account, and the majority of the women who make for ideal integrated healthcare patients are reachable through Facebook, Instagram, and email strategies.

Getting your daily posts into the newsfeed for free is becoming harder and harder, but the effectiveness of paid ads is still very strong, at least at the time of this writing. So, for now, be prepared to spend money to get your posts in front of your ideal target demographic. If you're new to ad targeting, be sure to get help and start small.

You shouldn't need to pay more than $1,000-$2,000 a month for someone who is great at generating online leads. Whoever they are, be it an agency, consultant, or part-time hire, make sure they have experience with medical lead generation in your niche *(and the laws surrounding it).*

Whether you boost a post or run an ad, your primary goal is to tell stories to attract interest and to acquire email addresses to build your email list.

Stories will get you more likes, clicks, and shares, which can make even an inexpensive boost more effective. Just don't forget to end every story with a "what to do next" (like sign up for a trial offer or join your newsletter list), or you'll waste your marketing dollars just entertaining people.[2]

[2] Be sure to understand and comply with all the channels' rules and State and National laws.

To review, here is the primary focus for your online marketing:

1. Create a compelling free simple lead offer to explain what results you get people by giving them the basic lifestyle changes they can make on their own.

2. Build a growing list of subscribers for your weekly email newsletter.

3. Run Social Media ads to attract new leads.

OUR MOST EFFECTIVE OFFLINE MARKETING

As we already mentioned, you're marketing to people who have often been abandoned and abused by traditional medicine. And now, you have the opportunity (and responsibility) to say something that's going to change their minds and get them back to enjoying life.

Not only are you hoping to improve on your own success by doing that, but their friends, family, and loved ones are likely hoping someone will get their attention, too.

To do that will often require a deeper engagement than you can get through a Facebook post.

You don't convince a 46-year-old to invest in a transformative care option based on an inspirational quote, morning workout video, or a holiday discount offer.

You need stories, the time to tell stories, and the ability to capture someone's full "listening" attention. That's most effectively done offline.

Pay attention now.

What I'm about to share is proven to be very effective—especially when I show you how to work these things together at once.

Speak to Local Groups as Often as You Can

This one may be the hardest tactic if you don't like public speaking. But it's definitely a profitable use of your time, so don't turn away just yet.

Your goal is to get as many guest speaking opportunities as you can so you can meet your ideal patients in a situation where you're a featured authority (not just a salesperson or another doctor!).

It takes years to master your keynote presentations. Starting small with your local rotary and membership clubs is a great way to develop your skills and still make an impact.

You'll learn to watch your audience to see when they lean in or when their eyes are starting to gloss over. You'll discover the right balance between emotion, stories, and science. These things take time and practice.

Start small. Your speech doesn't have to be an elaborate presentation. You're just looking for 10 to 30-minute opportunities to share a few stories, teach people about real healthcare, and then invite them to take the next step.

Connecting with people face-to-face is what's most important.

Even a five-minute speech is longer than an average website visit or YouTube video view, and it is MUCH more effective!

The easiest way to start is by asking your current patients if they're a member of any clubs or organizations that invite guest speakers. If they are, request an email introduction to the club's organizer or program director.

You'll be surprised how many groups there are in your area that are looking for health-related guest speakers. Here's a list of ideas to get you going:

Civic Groups
Philanthropic Groups
Rotary, Kiwanis, Lions, Elks, etc.
Retirees Clubs
Church Groups
Men's or Women's Groups
Business Lunch-and-Learns
4H Homemakers
Quilting/Knitting Clubs
Corporate Businesses
Non-Competing Medical Groups
American Diabetes Foundation
American Heart Association
Parkinson's & MS Support Groups
Arthritis & Joint Replacement Support Groups
Health Education Centers
Cardiovascular Health Clinics
Rehab Centers
Home Care Organizations
Caregiver Support Groups
Synergistic Businesses

In my experience, these groups are often smaller than 15–20 people at a time, so it's easy to connect on a personal level—and not that scary.

For most of these groups, the targeting is pretty specific as well, so finding your ideal audience is pretty easy.

Just get the contact information for the program director and send them a short, friendly email offering to speak to their members about optimal health and longevity for adults over 30, or people with Parkinson's, or joint pain, etc.

Whenever you can, try to niche the topic just a bit for the audience, and you'll be more likely to get an invitation to speak.

If you know a member of the group, be sure to share that in your email.

Join a Business Networking Group

At first, most doctors think that business-to-business (B2B) networking is a waste of time. That's a costly misconception.

We've been a member of a local B2B networking groups for 10 years, and we've tracked well over $1,000,000 in new patients and business directly from the groups. One of the first hires I made was a business development director to go out into the community to network, arrange speaking opportunities, and generate consultations for me because I was nervous about networking and it wasn't a strength at the time.

Networking groups offer access to three audiences at once:

First, you get access to the members themselves, many of whom are probably over 40 and good candidates for your services because they're busy business owners neglecting their own health.

Second, those business owners have employees, and you can arrange special offers for those employees and their family members as an "employee benefit" that costs the employer nothing except maybe hosting a lunch-and-learn for you.

Third, those business owners are well connected in the community. Once you teach them what you do and the specific referrals you're looking for, they become your marketing team.

A networking group is also a good support community to help you keep abreast of upcoming community events and small groups you may want to plug into—things like health fairs, aging-in-place conferences, caregiver events, etc.

With rare exceptions, every community has a couple of different business-to-business networking groups. Your local Chamber of Commerce is a good start. BNI (Business Networking International) is one of the most common in the US.

If you want to grow your business fast, block the time on your calendar and get involved in a strong networking group.

And don't forget to be a responsible, active member. Networking groups work when people know you're there to support them as well. When you give as much as you receive (or more!), these people can become great friends in your community.

Run a Direct Mail Postcard Campaign

If you think postcard mailings are dead or don't work, think again. Many of our high-ticket ideal patients live in golf communities or affluent neighborhoods. We started direct-mailing postcards to just those targeted areas suspecting we'd find patients who fit our practice, and it worked.

So, what's the secret to a postcard campaign?

Repetition.

You can't just send one and be done.

We teach clients to send three postcards over a 30-day period. Repetition is a key part of the plan because the first one almost always goes into the recipient's trash.

It's the THIRD consecutive postcard that produces the biggest response.

Most stop at one, maybe two, and then they say, "I tried that, and it didn't work."

If that's you, try again with three postcards spaced inside a 30-day period. We prefer using these cards to invite them to a transformation seminar where we have the opportunity to connect and educate our ideal patients.

Putting together your campaign isn't that hard either.

The U.S. Postal Service (USPS) makes it easy and affordable to do this with their Every Door Direct Mail (EDDM) offering. Canada has a similar service called Canada Post Neighbourhood Mail, and I suspect other countries do as well.

These services allow you to pick neighborhood routes with targeting information that is almost as detailed as what is available for Facebook ads. You simply go to the USPS website and research which neighborhoods (or mail routes) are most likely to have your ideal clients based on age, household income, interests, and more.

The system tells you how many homes are on your preferred route(s), and then you work with your local printer to design and address postcards to the homes for as little as 18 cents each.

Of course, there's a bit more to the process, but it's surprisingly easy to do. And most printers are now EDDM certified, which means they'll handle most of the details for you.

Best of all, you should be able to run the whole campaign, printing, postage, and all for about 50¢ a home per run!

Totally affordable, easily repeatable, and it works!

Just be sure to send all three postcards to the same route within 30 days. You can stay within a smaller budget by just doing one route at a time.

GET YOUR PROTOCOL BOOK DONE

The final idea is a biggie, and, when combined with the earlier ideas, makes everything much more effective.

We already discussed how a Protocol Book can be a gamechanger in your marketing. As we lay out these other marketing options, like the social media and postcard campaigns, you can see how having a call to action to "Request a free copy of our book on ___" could be a very attractive offer:

- Being an author makes you stand out as an expert above your unpublished peers.
- People want to work with the most respected experts.
- People research their options before they buy.
- Books let you tell a lot of stories.
- Books prepare and prequalify people for their first meeting with you.
- Books don't feel salesy.
- Books don't get thrown in the trash like business cards or fliers.

Just consider how much attention you've already invested in reading this book…and how that affects your understanding of how I can help you.

A book has remarkable longevity. It's waiting to tell your story whenever someone is ready to listen.

That's not something a business card or flier can do for you.

It's especially helpful for generating referrals. People (and your medical peers) are also much more likely to give someone your book than a business card or flier. It makes them feel good to give someone a real gift with inherent retail value.

Having a book makes all your other marketing efforts more effective:

- It's easier to get speaking engagements when you're a published author.
- It's easier to get attention on social media when people are talking about you and your book.
- It's easier to get your patients to refer you by giving friends your book.
- It's easier to get people to subscribe to your newsletter list with a book as your free giveaway.
- It's faster and easier to close a sale when a prospect has read your book.

Here's the really good news: **you don't even need to sit at a desk for weeks writing your book yourself!**

We've got a lot of the core content already written for you and available through our partner, Niche Pressworks.

For now, just imagine how having a Protocol Book and a Bestselling Signature Book could help you change a lot more lives faster.

Tell Them Exactly What to Do Every Step

I've learned something very important about marketing in the healthcare industry that's a bit different from other spaces: you *have* to tell people what you want them to do next. In some ways, that's true for any industry but imagine ending an office visit without providing a patient with any next steps—that visit won't really mean much in the long run.

It's the same thing with marketing and sales. If someone found you via your website, or a speaking engagement, or a postcard, what is it that you want them to do next? When I got started with content marketing, I was good at sharing stories, but I lost a lot of potential by not always including a clear call-to-action.

Whether you're engaging with a patient out in the world or in an exam room, remember that they are talking to you because they have a problem they have yet to solve on their own. They look to you as an expert, and they want your advice.

You have to tell your audiences what to do next in every interaction. Walk them through the next steps. Make it simple.

If you want them to call and make an appointment, tell them that.

If you want them to read an article or consume a simple lead offer, give them the link.

If you don't give your audiences a next step, they *will* find one on their own. It just might not be the one you want for them.

CHAPTER 7

SELLING CASH & INTEGRATIVE MEDICINE

"Doc, I believe in you," says a patient sitting in your exam room. "You see my problems and know what's best for me. You understand my symptoms and tell me what to do, and because you know best I will listen."

You may never encounter a patient who puts this sentiment into so many words, but the truth is, as a physician, you have this power. When you are in a position to give your patients honest insights and true, life-changing treatments, your confidence says more than your words ever could. This concept is called "transference of feeling." Your energy matters. When you believe a treatment is what's best for your patient, even if it was you or your family member in their situation, that person will follow you. They'll share your passion and conviction with their friends and family, too.

I've written a lot about marketing in this book, and now we're going to shift gears and talk about sales. When done right, the sales work you do for your practice will feel more like that conversation with a trusting patient in your exam room than any sales pitch you've ever seen before.

And while I could talk about this until I'm blue in the face, this is one point where I turn to lessons learned from my beloved game of rugby. I play that game because it teaches me so much about competition, but also about *cooperation*. Just as we fight for the ball in a scrum, our teammates and the opposing team also hold us up in the struggle. When you realize we are all playing the healthcare game together we can look at our differences and unique talents, and work together through "coopetition" (cooperation and competition) to change lives. Not one of us has the comprehensive solution or abilities to handle all aspects of our patient's health journey. When you can't pass the ball or recommend other services that will help your patient, you are either making it about you, or you're a ball hog.

That's what my friend and partner Phil Kaplan has done for me. Our shared history of health challenges brought us together and his delivery of our vital message awes me. I can't think of anyone better than Phil to speak to the need of independent healthcare providers to stand up, support each other, and start selling, and that's why I'm turning this chapter over to him.

"ADDRESSING THE PLIGHT OF THE PHYSICIAN ENTREPRENEUR: WHY DOCTORS NEED TO SELL...NOW"

By Phil Kaplan, CEO of T.R.U.E.

Most doctors who enter their own practices are more connected to a calling for helping others than by a burning desire to be a salesperson, to manage payroll, and to take on the stresses of an entrepreneurial business owner. In order, however, to find reward in bettering lives, the entrepreneurial element becomes more a need than a passion. Thus, most physicians in private practice might be referred to as "reluctant entrepreneurs."

As a business owner, you're aware of the importance of change. Attitudes change, approaches change, and the playing field seems to change faster than ever before.

We might view the process of ongoing change as an evolution.

Watching the medical field evolve, we marvel at the technology, the science, and the advances we have access to both as humans and as practitioners. It's reassuring to know that replacing a joint is now a viable option, and stimulating regeneration of tissue is no longer science fiction.

As a physician, marveling at advances is understandable. As a reluctant entrepreneur, the marvel leaves you less than fulfilled. Here's why.

You learn to build your business in a given demographic, with a particular promise, and with an offer that you feel presents a fair value exchange.

Assuming the promise and the offer prove viable, others see the impact, and the field becomes clamored with purveyors of solutions for the "problem" or the "need" for which you have the "fix." Even if you become the top practitioner in your field with the greatest market share, unless you evolve, inevitably the market you own becomes diluted.

It's time the aspiring leaders of this industry concurrently seek personal fulfillment (emotional and financial reward married to an undying sense of significance) and production. I don't only mean "productivity," as in the case of examining x number of patients, conducting y number of procedures, or writing z number of prescriptions. I mean production.

Every entrepreneur understands production. If, for the moment, we step aside from "The Calling," and become honest enough to admit we want to feel great about everything we do, we have to remove the reluctance and embrace the power we have to produce.

Every business owner knows *money in* has to exceed *money out*. Every business owner knows profit is the number of dollars left after expenses. Every business owner also knows, unless there's an annual, monthly, weekly focus on production, it's quite possible to sell your wares or work your magic and fail to see a justifiable reward.

It's precisely for this reason that a physician in practice needs to learn to market, to persuade, and while we may hate the word, to sell.

If you do, in fact, hate the word "sales," it isn't the concept you hate. It's what we've come to associate with it.

If the word itself summons up a vision of the car salesman, the well-dressed man or woman who comes into your office trying to sell you office supplies, or the "closer" in a real estate office or retail store, you're going to naturally have a distaste for the association.

If, on the other hand, you realize that acquiring a patient requires getting a prospective patient to say "yes," you'll come to realize that **the lifeblood of your emotional and financial fulfillment is directly tied to your ability to create those "yes" responses.**

In other words, your fulfillment is intrinsically linked to your willingness and your ability to integrate selling into the day-to-day, without stress, without pressure, and with a forever sense of morality.

Selling is good. It creates the proverbial win-win. You provide a patient with a life less riddled by pain, and you are rewarded fairly. Break the association you may have with selling and recognize there's a way to persuade others to make the best choices for themselves without ever running into limiting price resistance or buyer's remorse. As long as you deliver what you promise, the patient is happy on the other side of the "yes."

With full acceptance now of our need to sell, let's go back and re-examine the evolution of the medical field. If we trace the growth of Western medicine, we'd have to go back to ancient Greece where Plato, Socrates, and Hippocrates found "cures" in balancing interventions that addressed the body, the spirit, and in some ancient writings, the soul.

As you read this, you're aware a great many in need have become uncomfortable with "the medical paradigm" as it has evolved since ancient days. They may opt for "alternatives" and chase paths along which they'll find blends of Eastern medicine and spiritual healing. Perhaps people are longing for a lost "art" of medicine. Perhaps science has moved us too far away from empowerment and natural healing.

Here's a conversation stopped. Personal trainers can cure disease. You can argue it, but I'll present a strong argument.

If "cure" means "restore to health," and "disease" is movement away from ease (a literal dis-ease), we have to admit that a shift in movement (exercise) and nutrition can help a great many rediscover health. I'm not suggesting you leave medicine and pursue a personal training certification, but I am suggesting we're in a time where personal empowerment is available and in demand. If a practitioner was connected with a resource for exercise, nutrition, mindset, and spirit, it's quite likely he or she would have a much easier platform from which to "sell" to the masses.

This is a time to consider the space that lies between fitness and medicine, the opportune field that can draw those in need into a place closer, in theory, to their own comfort levels. This may be the most opportune space in business today.

It's hard to sell "what you do" to an audience jaded by the perception, flawed or otherwise, of the medicine you practice.

Here too, a perspective shift is in order. When prospective patients go elsewhere, they aren't rejecting you. They're confused. They're in need. They're in pain, and if you have a solution, there's no better time than right now to sell that pain, and if — and this is a *big* if—the pain relief you "sell" comes along with empowerment, you're about to start mining some new gold.

If we really zero in on the thread that runs through all of the misconceptions, fear, misinformation, and apprehension related to the conventions of medicine, we'll recognize it as a desire for change. As evidenced by public outcry and the political landscape, "let's change healthcare" is the underlying message. Few would contradict the thought that healthcare needs to be changed. The question is, "Who will change it?" In this question lies your greatest opportunity.

If people seek change, they're tired of convention. They have formed their own associations of the medical paradigm, and they want something different, something they perceive as better. Be the perceived pioneer who initiates that change, and from that position, "sell" the "yes."

It will require a bit of introspection to determine how you marry patient examination and assessment, communication, treatment, empowerment, and follow-up, but it's far and away the best use of your time in facilitating the next chapter in your practice.

While the word *wellness* has been thrown around for decades, with little in the way of proven magnetic appeal, our patients want to be "well." Ultimately "excellence" might be a goal, but "well" is a milestone, and if a patient is too sick, injured, or compromised to see "well" around the next corner, "better" becomes the next vital milestone.

Sell not the procedure, sell the outcome.

In this time of limitless purported options, your future patients want a guiding light. They want to understand that you have their best interest in mind. They want to understand that you have the ability to help them springboard past the immediate need, as your joint desire is "excellence."

Once you decide on your course, your promise, and the offer that meets the newly emerging marketplace, you can secure your position at the top of the field. Empower everyone you professionally touch, treat every patient as the most important person in the world, "sell" them what they want and deliver what they both want and need. Fearlessly exude your compassion and humanity, and you will fast find the reward and significance you always knew was possible.

At HealthOvators, we talk a lot about how often doctors make the mistake of marketing their services or a treatment plan instead of the outcomes or the transformation they deliver.

The reality is that the more frustrated a patient is, the less interested they are in coverups and managing their care.

These patients are interested in living the life they didn't think was possible any longer. *That* is what you are selling. You are not selling treatments, but the outcomes of your protocol. So, when you sit down with a prospect, you have to listen for their interests, their goals, their dreams, and what they really want. These are what we call their NLW's: Needs, Likes, and Wants.

If we can figure out what they really like to do and want to do, the job of selling procedures, and treatment plans just got way, way easier—because we're only selling the procedures, we know will give our patients what they want. But this means you first have to listen, ask questions, conduct a thorough assessment, and only then present a solution that meets their needs, likes, and wants.

I learned the hard way after nearly 10 years of marriage: to make my wife feel heard and understood, all I had to do was repeat nearly exactly what she said. That's ultimately what we're doing when we sell to our patients.

With this approach, you really aren't selling a treatment protocol at all. You are helping them choose what program is going to serve their life goals the best.

You become their health care manager, partner, and solution provider, instead of someone selling them another treatment to try.

Selling Without Selling

I used to hate marketing and sales because I felt like they were sleazy means to persuade people to give me their money. Then my mentors started asking me some really good questions and allowed me to form my own new beliefs about sales and marketing.

They also provided me with scripts that had nothing to do with manipulation, hard tactics, or deceptive practices. They showed me an approach to sales that was just about listening to what a prospective patient wanted.

Once I learned the script for selling fitness, regen medicine, and functional medicine, I was able to combine everything I learned and create the *Selling Without Selling* system. I use this system to train doctors to ethically and happily sell their life-changing programs with the help of questionnaires that show us *exactly* what patients are asking for.

Take a look at the patient intake form example on the next page. We created this for Katalyst in Missouri. By asking patients about the *outcomes* they are interested in before even performing an exam, it gives providers at Katalyst invaluable insight into how they can serve their patients best using their “Pain Resolution” treatment plan.

Then they perform their exam, consider treatment plans, and prescribe an outcome-based plan based on what the patient has already said they want. It’s *selling,* yes, but it doesn’t feel like a sales pitch. It feels like a *conversation*, one that tells the patient we are truly interested in listening and helping.

How much easier would it be to sell patients on the value of cash-based programs in this context? That’s what I mean when I talk about *Selling Without Selling.*

KATALYST
PAIN MANAGEMENT AND RESTORATIVE TREATMENT CENTER

PLAN QUESTIONS

P Procedures and Prescriptions

1.	Does pain interfere with your daily life?	YES / NO
2.	Has surgery been recommended for an orthopedic issue?	YES / NO
3.	Do you feel like you should perform at a higher level?	YES / NO
4.	Is pain an emotional burden for you?	YES / NO
5.	Are you looking for non-surgical and drug free options to better manage or resolve your pain?	YES / NO

L Lifestyle and Learning

6.	Do you have consistent strategies to manage your stress?	YES / NO
7.	Do you have a supportive spouse/family/friend to help you with your health journey?	YES / NO
8.	Does pain affect your ability to fall asleep, stay asleep and your energy throughout the day?	YES / NO
9.	Do you currently take daily supplements to optimize your health?	YES / NO
10.	Do you feel informed on the cause or trigger surrounding you pain?	YES / NO
11.	Have you undergone testing recommended by a provider such as hormone, heavy metal, or genetics testing?	YES / NO

PAGE 1 | WWW.KATALYSTMD.COM | 314-230-7800 | CARETEAM@KATALYSTMD.COM
KATALYST MEDICAL, LLC | 7000 BAXTER ROAD, SUITE 200 CHESTERFIELD, MO 63005

An example of gaining important outcome-based information on the patient intake form. Created for Katalyst Pain Management & Restorative Treatment Center.

CHAPTER 8

HOW TO IMPLEMENT IDEAS ... FAST!

By now, you may be feeling a bit overwhelmed by these ideas and how you'll get them implemented. Most independent doctors come to us doing way too much stuff that they shouldn't be doing, which is keeping them from their real income potential.

If you're still doing all the patient care yourself, and all the bill paying, inventory, posting to Facebook, hiring, firing, housework…you're going to remain stuck in an awful version of an Entrepreneurial Groundhog Day repeating the same events over and over and over.

In order to grow past 100 employees, I had one rule: get hired, document your job, become great at it, hire your replacement at a more affordable rate, train them to do it and then follow up to see if they are still doing all aspects at a high level.

The only way to grow to medical thought leader status is to become one of the few in the world who do what you do best. You need top talent that are growers that will help your vision become a reality.

You've got to get out from under the day-to-day operations, establish yourself as a true BUSINESS OWNER, and focus on what's most important: bringing in patients.

One of the greatest values of joining HealthOvators is that you get to spend time with doctors who've overcome the scarcity mindset and are growing a scalable practice, enjoying more independence, and making more money—a lot faster than before.

That experience is life-changing. You learn to see the opportunities around you differently. Building your practice becomes something you really enjoy because you're getting more done and seeing results.

For information about joining HealthOvators, including our next live event dates and location, visit HealthOvators.com

FREE UP YOUR TIME

To realize this vision of rising above the day-to-day, the first thing you need to do is free up some time … FAST!

Grab a pen and paper right now and start writing down all the repetitive tasks you're doing regularly. Which ones could you stop or delegate to someone else?

Hire a college student to do laundry and clean equipment. If you've got staff who works for you, give them additional responsibilities between sessions. Perhaps one of your first patients would like to work for you to earn a discount or keep the bargain rate they've had for way too long.

We've got HealthOvators members who've traded coaching time for training, graphic design, cleaning, bookkeeping, even marketing.

When we first started accepting patients, we did everything. But as time went on and our patient list grew, we got to a point where there weren't enough hours in the day for us to take care of it all. At this point, we made it a priority to hire reliable staff so we could get out into the community and get patients. We scaled up from there and launched two other profitable joint ventures—including HealthOvators!

It starts with thinking differently.

Back to you and your time.

Look at your patient schedule. Can you condense your schedule or rearrange it to give you one business development day a week?

Can you combine several private patients into small group visits? Moving just four to five individual patients to a group program could free up anywhere from three to five hours of your time per week! They get a discount and new accountability buddies; you get some time to work on bringing in more patients.

Yes, change is scary. Do it anyway. Start thinking out of the box and get your time back FAST.

After all, time is money.

THINK RETURN ON INVESTMENT

When you're investing your marketing dollars, think of a slot machine with a guaranteed payout. Would you put $1 in if you knew it would give you $10 out?

Marketing works like that. You invest money in the places that are proven effective, and your investment comes back in the form of patient contracts that pay you much more in return!

For example, would you invest $300 in a one-year BNI membership for the opportunity to get 10 good referrals worth $300 per month each?

Or, would a $500 investment in printing and postage for a 3-time postcard campaign be worth it if it yields you three new clients worth over $10,800 per year?

The point is, you spend money to make money. Invest wisely in ideas that others, like us, have already proven to work.

The ones who are the most successful when they have a proven marketing return on investment spend more than the competition. My goal is to spend as much as I can operationally handle because it only makes sense.

One of my mentors, Ed Rush, says, "You can't cheap your way to massive success."

There's no need to experiment here or to start from scratch. We've already shared in depth what's working for us and our clients and private practices.

Now, we want to help you implement those ideas FASTER.

TAKE ADVANTAGE OF PRACTICE MANAGEMENT AND MARKETING SOLUTIONS

One of the biggest advantages we offer our HealthOvators members is a community. It's not easy being a black sheep or viewed as outside the box as a medical professional. But together, we're learning to navigate a growing market and sharing everything we learn along the way.

Having access to this caliber of professional services specific to the integrative healthcare market is a MAJOR competitive advantage:

- Group and 1-1 Coaching Packages
- On-Site Consulting
- Leadership Adventure Retreats
- Libraries of On-Demand Video Training
- Done-for-You Forms, Lead Offers, Emails, and more
- Brand Building, Email and Website Services
- Bestseller Book Coaching & Publishing
- Celebrity Speaker Coaching and Media Training
- Sales Training Systems
- Mastermind Events
- Vendor Discounts and Group Purchasing Opportunities

These services all represent best practices that I had to learn the hard way, one mistake at a time. But today's integrative healthcare market is maturing. We understand what works and what doesn't, and that means you have the opportunity to skip right ahead and start building your practice—fast.

CHAPTER 9

WHAT IMPACT WILL YOU HAVE?

Let's close by talking about what happens if you don't give it all you've got to share your skills and your knowledge with the world.

Are you the best at what you do? Do you transform lives? Do you know what you're doing? Someone who is not the best, does not deliver on outcomes, and doesn't know what they are doing is taking money from the people you can help.

You can't stay the best-kept secret. In truth, to do so would be selfish. We need your competition! We need your cooperation! "Coopetition," as I call it, is needed to change the world. Even if we may have some overlap, there are more than enough people waiting for our help. We need to say, "Cheers!" to the fact that we were called to contribute to a purpose bigger than ourselves. Health is the greatest wealth, and it's time to share that wealth with as many as we can.

THINK DIFFERENTLY

What if you had the ability to *actually* do what you do best? What if you really practiced medicine that transforms lives? What if all your time was spent sharing your mission, your greatest passion and skill? What if you were able to practice when and where you wanted? What if you were to choose the exact life you wanted?

What will happen to the person whose life you change? What major life accomplishments are ahead of them because of what you do? How much money does good health generate for their family? What does health do for their family's joy and happiness? What does it do for yours?

The cost of not figuring this out is too great to bear.

If you have read this far, it's because you know you can change lives. You were born to make a difference.

Don't let fear hold you back. Don't let money hold you back. Don't let skeptics hold you back. Don't let lack of priority and clarity to hold you back from your purpose in this world. Sometimes—and just maybe sometimes—your excuse not to do something is the very reason you need to do it. As a medical professional, you're smart enough to know that if you don't do something differently, expecting a different result would be foolish.

So, if you don't have the money, time, or know-how, that's exactly the reason you hire a coach for help. It's hypocritical to ask a patient to invest in your life-changing services if you're not investing in your own progress and impact.

The reason we believe you can do this is because we have done it. We were not marketers. We had a bleeding heart to help people just like you. And because of that, we have helped hundreds of health and wellness professionals and practices do it without all the painful mistakes we have already made.

We need you to step up. Stop pointing the finger at big pharma, the government, insurance companies, and administrators.

If you're not part of the solution, you're part of the problem.

We need HealthOvators just like you to help create a world our loved ones not only can live in, but thrive in. Join us in our efforts to help life-changing health leaders attract, convert and retain cash-paying patients, so you can treat those patients with lifestyle, functional, and regenerative medicine solutions that actually restore and regenerate health. Do this while building a practice that provides you with the impact, income, and independence you deserve.

Get started today: HealthOvators.com and JRBurgessConsulting.com

CUSTOMIZED PRACTICE BLUEPRINT AND RESOURCE LIBRARY
PERSONAL
PRIVATE FACEBOOK GROUP
5 PILLARS OF PRACTICE SUCCESS

Made in United States
North Haven, CT
05 November 2026

21772057R00050